German Twin-Engine Bombers of World War II

Manfred Griehl

Schiffer Publishing Ltd

1469 Morstein Road, West Chester, Pennsylvania 19380

SOURCES

Federal Archives
German Museum
Dornier Archives
FL Archives
Heinkel Archives
Henschel Archives
MBB Archives
Radinger Collection
Selinger Collection
Author's Archives

Key to the Title Page

1. Oil cooler
2. Ring cooler
3. Cooler flaps
4. Jumo 211 motor
5. Instruments
6. Retractable landing gear
7. Cockpit
8. Control stick
9. Control system
10. Releasable cockpit canopy
11. Tracer-bullet case
12. RAB (Sequential bomb-release apparatus)
13. Aiming device
14. Belly pan
15. A-position 15 machine gun
16. B-position 15 machine gun
17. C-position 15 machine gun
18. Antenna mast
19. Antenna
20. Emergency antenna
21. Tailfin
22. Rudder with trimming flap
23. Stabilizer
24. Elevator
25. Trimming flap for elevator
26. Retractable tail wheel
27. First-aid kit
28. Rubber raft
29. Fuel quick-release
30. Oxygen tanks for high-altitude breathing apparatus
31. Master compass
32. Direction finder
33. Trailing antenna
34. Forward bomb bay
35. Rear bomb bay
36. Cargo carrier
37. Fuel tank
38. Oil reservoir
39. Landing flap
40. Aileron
41. Trimming flap for aileron
42. Navigation light (port)
43. Pressure jet
44. Diving brake (2-part)
45. Landing light
46. Anti-icing system
47. Variable-pitch propeller
48. Landing gear flaps

PHOTO CREDITS

Dornier GmbH (12), Creek (4), Dressel (3), Aerial History Research Group (16), Heck (4), Henschel GmbH (1), Heinkel GmbH (9), Lange (1), Lutz (9), Messerschmitt-Bölkow-Blohm (2), Menke (2), Nowarra (6), Radinger (8), Rohrbach (2), Schliephake (5), Seebrandt (2), Selinger (2), Stapfer (4), Wittigeyer (1), Author (8).

Translated from the German by Dr. Edward Force.
Copyright © 1989 by Schiffer Publishing, Ltd.
Library of Congress Catalog Number: 89-84173.

Printed in the United States of America.
ISBN: 0-887408-191-0
Published by Schiffer Publishing Ltd.
1469 Morstein Road, West Chester, Pennsylvania 19380

Please write for a free catalog.
This book may be purchased from the publisher.
Please include $2.00 postage.
Try your bookstore first.

FOREWORD

All earlier volumes about German twin-engine bombers of the armed forces are out of print. To satisfy the demand, we have thus decided to put out a special volume about these models. Care has been taken that no illustrations repeat those of the earlier books.

The Editors

A HE 111 H-6 of the 2nd/KG 54 on an operational flight, 1942.

ORIGINS

Proceeding the positive operational experiences of the fighter and bomber squadrons of the German High Command in World War I, the first step in building up the new Luftwaffe was to include ten bomber and auxiliary bomber detachments.

At Berlin-Tempelhof, therefore, "Bomber Squadron 1" was set up as of January 1934, disguised as the "Traffic Inspection of the German Lufthansa". From this there later developed Auxiliary Fighter Squadrons 172 and 274. At first these units were equipped with JU 52 trimotors. What followed was the steady formation of new detachments and units of the organizations. During the next few years a slow but sure change to Do 11, Do 13 and Do 23, and later to Ju 86 and the faster Do 17 and He 111 took place. The "Gotha and Giebelstadt Battle Regiments" were formed as of the spring of 1935; from them, there subsequently developed such famous squadrons as the KG 4 "General Wever" and KG 76. As of 1938 the KG 254 was built up, later to become the nucleus of the "Death's-head" KG 54. KG 254 was organized as of 1938 in Langendiebach and Giessen. From this, there later developed a portion of KG 155, which in May of 1939 became the well-known "Griffin Squadron" KG 55. The "Alpine Squadron" was formed from portions of KG 255, and was later renumbered KG 51, while its second unit became the 3rd/KG 77.

In August of 1939 there were already thirteen fighting squadrons, though not all were fully equipped. Also being organized were the Ju 88 instructional unit and the Aerial Intelligence Unit 100, which flew Ju 52 and He 111 planes and became the nucleus of all future target-locating units.

Thus 30 battle groups existed in all, of which more than 21 were fully equipped with the He 111. Nine units used the Do 17. Only parts of the "Hindenburg Fighter Squadron" still had the Ju 86.

Other than the operational models named here, there were also many other twin-engined warplanes, not all of which went beyond the testing phase.

For example, the Ju 36 and 37, developed in Sweden, whose performance was just as unimpressive as that of the Do N and the Do Y, the latter rebuilt with twin engines and also called Do 15.

Shortly after the introduction of the Do 11 and 13, the improved Do 23, powered by two **BMW VIU** engines, was delivered to the troops in large numbers. This plane first flew on September 1, 1934 and had a top speed of 260 kph.

The Dornier had a range of 1350 km and could climb to a maximum altitude of 4200 meters. This high-wing monoplane had fixed landing gear, in contrast to the Do 13, which first flew on February 13, 1933. Thus it also differed from the Do F (Do 11) "Mail and Freight Plane", which had its first flight in May of 1932.

Less successful too were the light twin-engine Henschel bombers, such as the Hs 124 or 127, which came into being on account of orders for fighter-bombers. After only two test flights, no further orders for the Hs 127 came from the Air Ministry (RLM).

Ju K 37 Medium Bomber (S-RABP).

Upper left: Ju S 36 fighter (D-AMIX) with open B-position guns.

Upper right: Dornier Do 11 (Do F) with Siemens "Jupiter VI" motors. Without defensive armament.

Left: A Do 23.

Left: Do 23 bomber with two BMW VI motors.

Lower left: Training plane (army scout) Do 23 G, 1940.

Below: Hs 124 V2 light twin-engine bomber.

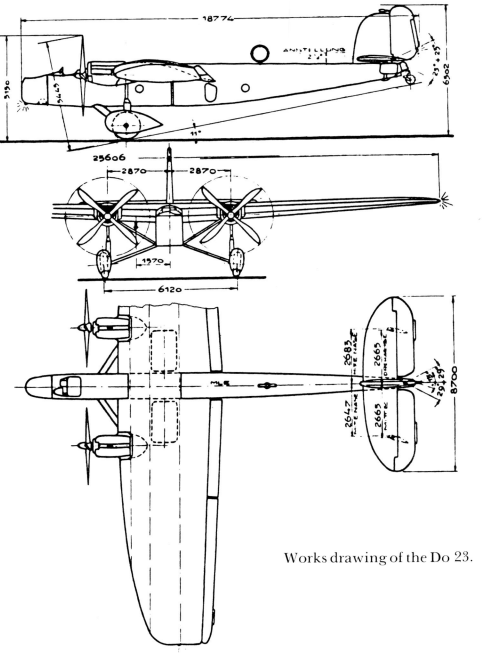

Works drawing of the Do 23.

The same thing happened to the Messerschmitt Bf 161 and 162. A total of only five models left the assembly shop, including both the Bf 161 V1 (D-AABA) and V2, plus the Bf 162 V1 through V3 with registrations D-AIXA, AOBE and AOVI. The planes were intended for use as "high-speed bombers, fighter-bombers and long-range reconnaissance planes". The test models fitted with DB 600 Aa powerplants could carry either ten 50-kg or two SC 250 bombs. The three-seater planes, carrying only two MG 15 guns in the nose and tail as defensive armament, corresponded to the usual standards. During flight testing in Augsburg it was learned by 1938 that neither the performance nor the potential payload met the requirements of the RLM.

Heinkel took seaplanes such as the He 59 and mounted two-wheel main landing gear, in order to test out the possibility of ground-supported operations. One goal was an uninterrupted continuation of testing during the winter months, when the Baltic Sea was usually frozen.

Despite its sturdiness, the big biplane could only be operated as a seaplane in areas where air superiority was held.

The time had come for high-speed bomb carriers such as the Do 17, as its debut at Dubendorf, near Zürich, in 1937 showed publicly, when a Do 17 flew away from the competition and caused great international astonishment.

Above: Messerschmitt Bf 162 V2, D-AOBE.

Left: Bf 161 V2 light bomber.

DORNIER DO 17 215

After being displayed in mock-up form, the Do 17 VI was finished in November of 1934 and flew for the first time on November 23 of that year. Because of the thoroughly good pilot evaluations of the first three test models, the RLM ordered eleven further models a year later. After the factory and weapons testing was finished in South Germany, as well as in Rechlin, the Dornier factory, and after building several additional test models, production began on the E and M series. The original models were the Do 17 V15 and 17 and MV2, which used DB 600 and BRAMO 323 motors. In 1937 the Dornier 17 P appeared, which was soon to become, along with the F version, the primary equipment of long-range reconnaissance units 10, 11, 14, 22 and 31.

The Dornier firm developed the Do 17 Z-1 to Z-10 production run as essentially improved and combat-strengthened operational planes. The first test model with the civilian registration D-ABVD, was to be followed in December 1939 by another 346 operational machines. On May 11, 1940 the number of Do 17 Z's on hand in the Luftwaffe added up to 422 planes. Most of them were used by fighter squadrons 2, 3, 76 and 77. After the zero series of ten planes with Z-1 numbers came the Z-2 command plane or "staff-echelon reconnaissance plane". The Do 17-Z4 was a blind-flying trainer, the Z-5 a sea fighter, and the Do 17 Z-6 version a pure weather plane.

Above: Do 17 MV1 model (Factory #691) D-AELE.

Below: Do 17 M-1 high-speed bomber with Bramo 323 A motors.

Right: Do 17 M-1 with diving brake; behind it the Do 17 V18 and a test model of the Do 17 Z.

Lower right: Operational plane of the Do 17 M-1 type, used by KG 2.

Below: Do 17 P weather plane at Rhein-Main Air Base.

Above: B-position gun and window mantlet of a Do 17 Z-2.

Upper right: A Do 17 Z-1 of the 4th/KG 77.

As a further development of the Do 17 Z, the Dornier firm went on to the Do 215, of which two test models (D-AFFY,D-AIIB) and a zero series of twelve machines with DB 601 A motors were made at first.

After a few planes of the Do 215 A-1 export-version type, Dornier produced the B-1 as a long-distance reconnaissance plane and the B-2 and B-3 as fighter planes with strengthened defensive armament. The Do 215 B-4 long-range reconnaissance planes in particular were produced in large numbers, most of which went into operation in the West.

Right: The DB 601 Aa motor of a Do 215 B-4.

DORNIER DO 217-317-417

The first flight of the Do 217 V1 took place over Upper Swabia on October 4, 1938. Thirteen test models and approximately 1500 series planes were to be produced until the summer of 1944, when production was halted in favor of fighter planes. The first two models were fitted with DB 601 A-1 motors, after which most were equipped with Jumo 211 A-1/A-2 powerplants, and from the Do 217 V8 on, generally the high-performance BMW 801 A-1. A portion of the planes belonged to the A-O and C-O production runs. The B-O version was dropped because of the bomber design with Jumo 211 B-1 motors; at first five zero-series planes were to be built (one machine of which was among the KG 2 fleet). A few Do 217 A-O were supplied to the Rowehl Reconnaissance Command, but were only in operation for a short time.

Actual large-series production began with the test models Do 217 V10 and V11, which can be regarded as the forerunners of the E-1 and E-2 production series. Approximately 300 of these planes came off the assembly lines in Friedrichshafen, Munich and Wismar. The mass of these bombers went to KG 2 and 40, which operated in Western Europe. The Do 217 E-4 was produced in the highest numbers of any E version, with over 250 bombers made. A portion of these "Atlantic Warplanes" intended mainly for over-sea operations and fitted with a 20 mm gun in the bow of the fuselage, were later rebuilt into guided missile carriers. The seventy Do 217 E-5 were designated "Warplanes for Special Operations" and were normally intended to carry one Hs 293 A-1 glider bomb and a large auxiliary tank to extend their range for anti-shipping attacks.

Above: Test model of the Do 217 V9 (CO+JM) in Löwenthal.

Below: Do 217 A-O during Dornier factory testing.

27257

Left: One of the zero-series Do 217 C-O planes with SC 50 dummies during Dornier loading testing.

Above: A night bomber of the 5th/KG 6 (3E+EN) in Northern France in the spring of 1943, just before going into operations.

Above: Do 217 E-2 during running-in.

Below: Do 217 E-5 "Special Warplane" of the 6th/KG 100 with Hs 293 A-1 glider bomb and auxiliary tank.

Right: Loading a Do 217 E-2 of KG 2.

Do 217 K-1 of the KG 6 target-locating unit.

The **Do 217 H** was planned as a low-level bomber, but did not go into series production; only three planes were built as flying powerplant test benches.

Three primary versions of the **Do 217 K** were also produced. The K-1 corresponded almost completely to the Do 217 E2/4 but had a cabin with all-around visibility to improve visual conditions. The low-level bomber version was developed into the Do 217 **K-2** and **K-3** guided missile carriers, with the large wing areas of the M-11. The planes could now include controllable PC 1400 X bombs in their payload. The **K-3** could carry either suspended glider bombs or controllable FX (Fritz X) bombs.

Right: Test model of Do 217 HV3 with DB 603 A motors.

At least 480 of the Do 217 M-1 to M-11 were made. The M-1 still resembled the K-1, though it had DB 602 motors instead of BMW 801. Various special types were built as torpedo bombers, high-altitude fighters and guided-missile carriers, or tested only in small numbers. The Do 217 M-9, for example, was given a triangular empennage, as is characteristic of the Do 317. Dornier produced the M-11 as the last series version of the Do 217 bomber; these planes were revised to serve as low-level bombers.

Most Do 217 K went into operation as bombers and "special fighters" with KG 2, 6 and 40, as well as KG100. Along with anti-shipping attacks over the Atlantic and Mediterranean, bombing runs on English cities, airfields and factories were the main targets of these units. The lack of air superiority determined the course of these very costly operations, which necessitated the new establishment of numerous individual units.

On the other hand, only a few models of the planned dive and torpedo bombers were built, for example, the Do 217 M-2 or R-1. A similar fate awaited the Dornier firm's Do 217 P high-altitude fighters. After two A-O had been equipped with DB 601 R and GM-1 systems, the Project Bureau and Construction Department developed the P-1, which derived from the E-2, as a high-altitude bomber with a pressurized cabin. At first six test models were to be built, of which the Do 217 PV1 (BK+IR) first flew on June 6, 1942 and later reached altitudes of up to 13,000 meters. The fourth P-model could even climb to 15,200 meters.

As a further development, in part with a completely new air-frame construction, Dornier suggested the Do 317 and 417.

Above: Do 217 M-1 (U5-LR, factory #722753) of the 7th/KG 2 in France, 1943.

Below: Side view of the Do 217 M-11 with PC 1400 X bombs.

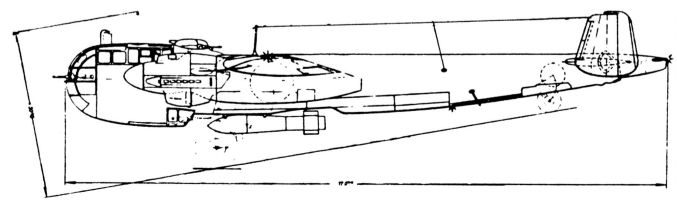

The Do 317, from which many plans were drawn, appeared only in the form of a single model, with VK-IY designation. The Fw 191 and Ju 288 has a greater power reserve, so that the RLM was more interested in the further development of these new bombers.

The Do 417, also called the "work plane", was meant to set completely new standards. After evaluating experiences with it over the ocean and on operations over England, a twin-engined, very tactically efficient, easy-to-produce fighter plane was to be made, to bring new life to the offensive operations of the Luftwaffe.

Above: Test model Do 317 V1 (VK+IY),in Löwenthal.

Right: Three views of the Do 417 project, the so-called "working plane".

HEINKEL HE 111

Building on the experience with high-speed aircraft gained from the He 70, the Heinkel firm produced the He 111, the first plane built in their new factory at Rostock-Marienehe, to a design by the well-known Günter brothers. The final construction was directed by Karl Schwärzler.

The He 111 a, later called He 111 V1, first flew on February 24, 1935. Its flying characteristics were fascinating. This was also true of the next three test models (D-ALIX, D-ALES and D-AHAO). While the V2 joined the German Lufthansa (DLH) fleet as the "Rostock" (He 111 C-0), the third He 111 became the prototype of the He 111 A-1, a bomber. The Lufthansa received other fast commercial planes as G-0, G-1 and G-3. The twin-engined He 111 G-5 bomber, on the other hand, was delivered to Turkey.

The young Luftwaffe was first given the improved He 111 B-1 version, while ten He 111 A-1 were exported to China. The first squadrons to be equipped with these fast warplanes were KG 152, 153 and 157. Meanwhile production of the B-2 version continued in Wismar. Some of these machines saw strenuous service with Battle Group K 88 during the Spanish Civil War. But until about 1942 the majority of the He 111 B were used as training planes. This was also true of the He 111 D-1, fitted with Jumo 211 engines; V6 (D-AXOH) was their model.

The next series production versions were types He 111 E-1 to E-4. V11 (D-ARCG) was their prototype. After testing at the front over Spain, the operational models were used by the squadrons for only a short time before they too were used as training

Above: The fourth test model of the He 111 (D-AHAO) during a display.

Below: Heinkel He 111 J-1 warplanes being serviced.

planes. The J and F versions are also worth noting; they were characterized by either a new wing shape or the capability of carrying torpedos. On September 19, 1938 there were 272 of the He 111 B, 171 of the He 111 E version, only 39 He 111 F and 88 He 111 J at hand. Out of a total of 570 He 111 planes, 468 were cleared for operations at that time. On September 2, 1939 there were only 59 of the He 111 E and J planes in use by battle groups. Meanwhile two large-series production runs, of He 111 P and H, were being built simultaneously.

Left: Loading a He 111 B-1 with SC 250 bombs.

Above: An early operational model of the He 111 H-6 in the West.

Below: He 111 H-5 of Coastal Air Unit 106.

Above: Heinkel 111 H-6 of Squadron 26.

Upper Right: Running-in at Heinkel, with a He 111 H-6 (DM+LE) in the foreground.

Right: Two He 111 H-16 of KG 53 in the East.

He 111 H-6 of the first unit of KG 26, the "Lion Squadron".

The He 111 B-0 (D-AQUO), as first model, was built with the new asymmetrical cabin affording all-around visibility. The He 111 V8 which resulted took its first flight in January of 1938. As the test model for the new stage C, the He 111 V23 (D-AHAY) was later added, though it still had the two-tier cabin. The Luftwaffe had 749 He 111 P and H planes in use in September of 1939, after the first model of the coming H versions, the He 111 V 19 (D-AUKY) was thoroughly convincing.

The He 111 H differed from the P mainly in its powerplant. The He 111 P, fitted with two DB 601 Aa motors, was built in six main versions. The relatively small zero series was followed as of the spring of 1939

by the P-1, which was capable of carrying a bomb load of 2000 kilograms. In the P-2 version, produced as of May 1939, Heinkel had modified the FT and exhaust systems. The P-3 was built in series as a training plane. The next version was designated He 111 P-4 and had one or two PVC (powder-electric suspension apparatus for cylindrical loads) and the usual ETC (electric vertical suspension). The last P version was the He 111 P-6 with two DB 601 N motors, each producing 1178 horse-power. A special version, the P-6/R2, was used as a towplane for freight gliders, and went out of production in 1940 along with the other P variations in favor of the He 111 H.

Series production of the He 111 H-0 began in May of 1939 and was based on the 19th test model, D-AUKY. The H planes were powered by Jumo 211 motors. The H-1 differed from the H-2 in terms of its oil coolers and Jumo 211 A-3 motors.

In the Polish campaign, He 111 P and H planes were used in the air fleets of squadrons 1, 3, 4, 26 and 27 as well as Training Squadron 1. The experiences gained there quickly led to a lasting strengthening of the defensive armament.

Operations over the North Sea and English coastal waters also took place before the planes of KG 26 were used, more frequently, for "armed long-range reconnaissance" in the sea war around the British Isles. After the occupation of Norway, in which the He 111 took part, and operations with Air Fleets 2 and 3 in the West, an He 111 first flew over the English mainland on June 18, 1940.

The He 111 H-4 and H-5 planes had an improved belly-pan as well as a changed bomb-releasing system. The stronger Jumo 211 F-1 motors, with 1340 horsepower each, were built in, beginning with the H-6. The defensive armament was increased to seven machine guns, and some planes also carried a 20 mm FF machine gun in order to attack ground targets effectively. The He 111 units were also given the task of laying aerial mines between August 8 and 12, 1940. They also took part in the costly aerial action during the Battle of Britain. After numerous Heinkel bombers had become victims of the English anti-aircraft guns in the daytime, the Luftwaffe command turned more and more to night-time bombing runs.

Attacks on targets in Southeastern Europe, Africa and the USSR followed. During the course of time special versions, such as the H-8 with a balloon-cable cutting apparatus, or the torpedo bombers, were built. The H-10 had even more powerful motors, the He 111 H-11 differed in having changed armament. Heinkel built the H-12 as carrier planes for the Hs 293. The H-14 was similar to the H-16 with its strengthened weapons system. The pathfinder plane (He 111 H-18) was followed by the H-20, which could be equipped for service as a drop plane for paratroopers, towplane for gliders, night bomber or intruder plane. The identifying mark of all versions from the He 111 H-20 on was the DL 131 revolving turret atop the middle of the fuselage.

Unlike them, the H-21 was powered by two Jumo 213 E-1 (1750-HP) motors. Heinkel developed the He 111 H-15 and H-22 as carriers for BV 246 and Fi 103. The last version was called H-23 and used as a transport plane. A few special versions also deserve mention, such as the He 111 V32, the model of a high-level bomber with DB 601 U motors, exhaust turbocharging and ring coolers, and planes with fixed tail guns or torpedo tubes for explosive charges meant to shake up enemy pursuit planes.

The Luftwaffe's last operations with the He 111 in 1945, for example on February 1, when six battle groups with a total of 445 planes attacked on the eastern front and destroyed or damaged more than 300 enemy vehicles. At the end of February 1945 the Luftwaffe still had 248 He 111 planes, plus an additional 66 as OKL reserves.

In April of 1945 the Testing Command 200 flew a few offensive operations with its He 111 and Do 217 guided missile planes. The hotly contested river crossings in the East were their targets.

Above: Low-level flight of a He 111 H-20 over Northern Italy in the spring of 1945.

Below: A crash-landed He 111 H-20 of the 1st/KG 27 in the East.

JUNKERS JU 86

The Ju 86 came into being in 1933 through the cooperation of the newly created C-office and the DLH. The first militarily usable example was the Ju 86 V5 (D-AHOE). It became the forerunner of the A-0 and A-1 production series, with which KG 152 was briefly supplied. After the B and C series were delivered to the DLH, Junkers presented the Ju 86 D-1 series, patterned on the sixth test model and powered by two Jumo 205 C-4 motors. Equipped with two BMW 132 F motors, the Ju 86 E-1 was supplied to, for example, KG 253. The Ju 86 E-0 (D-ALOH) served as a model. The Ju 86 V10, actually built identically to the E-2 version, became the forerunner of at least forty Ju 86 G-1 planes which were built in 1938. After many of the previous series-production planes had already been turned over to the B-schools, the G-1 version, with each of its two BMW 132 N motors producing 865 horsepower, offered a greater range of performance than the Ju 86 E-1 or E-2. Ju 86 planes saw their last operations in the supplying of Stalingrad. There 42 Ju 86's were lost between November 24, 1942 and February 3, 1943, seven of them being missing. Thirteen crashed during takeoffs and landings at various airfields, twenty were shot down or had to be written off for other reasons.

Upper right: Junkers Ju 86 A-1 and D-1 of Squadron 253 over Germany in 1936.

Right: A Ju 86 A-1 during operations in Spain.

Above: An operational Ju 86 E-1 of KG 253 coming in for a landing.

Above: A Ju 86 G-1 trainer, the school's command plane.

Below: A zero-series Ju 86 G-1 after an accident in Prague.

Below: A Ju 86 P-1 high-level bomber during testing in Dessau.

JUNKERS JU 88

The Ju 88, the Do 217 and the He 111 were the three standard bombers of the German Luftwaffe.

The first test model, the Ju 88 V1 (D-AQEN), first flew on December 21, 1936. The prototype was to be followed by 114 additional test models and some 9100 bombers, almost 4000 night fighters and about 2000 reconnaissance planes. Factory testing was carried out along with the V2 (D-ASAZ) and V4 (D-ASYI). The Ju 88 V5 "record plane" (D-ATYU) was also tested later with diving brakes and the lateral empennage of the Ju 288.

The Ju 88 V6 (KD+ME) flew as of June 18, 1938 as the model for the first large production series, the Ju 88 A-1. This was the first plane of the kind with a lengthened fuselage, larger high-altitude empennage and a second bomb shaft. On April 13, 1944 the plane crashed in Brandis. The Ju 88 V7 was introduced as the prototype for the next large series, which was designated A-5. This plane had improved defensive armament, with two single MG 15 machine guns in position B and greater wing surfaces. The first flight of D-ARNC, (later GU+AE) took place on September 27, 1938. The plane was later tested with four-bladed airscrews and finally rebuilt as a "high-speed transport plane".

From the Ju 88 V9 there grew the zero series of the Ju 88 A, beginning with factory number 0001. After later models had been built, there appeared the first Ju 88 A-5's (D-APSF) fitted with BMW 801 engines. The following test models were used, for example, to test the DVL safety controls and high-altitude use.

The first Ju 88A-4 linked to a large series was V21 (factory # 3113, D-ACBO, ND+BM),

Above: Cockpit mock-up of the planned Ju 85 bomber.

Below: Ju 88 V2 prototype (D-ASAZ, factory # 4942) in Dessau.

and first flew on November 1, 1940. Soon afterward the plane was tested with Jumo 213 motors.

The Luftwaffe accepted not only the Ju 88 A-1 and A-5 as series-production planes, but also the Ju 88 A-3 trainers with double controls and the A-6 version. The latter was an anti-balloon plane, in which form the Do 17 had also been tested, and the He 111 had gone into production. The A-7 provided another training plane, though it was based on the A-5.

The Ju 88 A-12 was also an A-5, but the cockpit had been widened and the defensive armament removed. There was one teardrop version each of the Ju 88 A-1 and A-5, designated A-9 and A-10, From test model V31 on, there followed a row of planes that were to carry on the further development of the production Ju 88 A-4. In addition to motor testers (V34 through V40), the Junkers firm also produced planes with lengthened wings, as well as a tropical version.

The Junkers Ju 88 A-4 became the "workhorse" of the squadrons and was armed with an 81 I machine gun in A position, two MG 81 I in B position, and one MG 81 Z in C position. The bomb-dropping system allowed the loading of two 1000-kilogram and two 500-kilogram bombs. The A-14 was later developed as a variant, differing from the A-4 by its Kuto nose. The teardrop type was designated A-11.

The Ju 88 D-1 through D-7 production runs were long-range reconnaissance planes, which were used by almost all the Luftwaffe's F-groups. The first series came into being through the rebuilding of A-1, A-4 and A-5 cells. The Ju 88 D-6 was a special version with BMW 801 J motors; the D-7 was another with an additional GM 1 system.

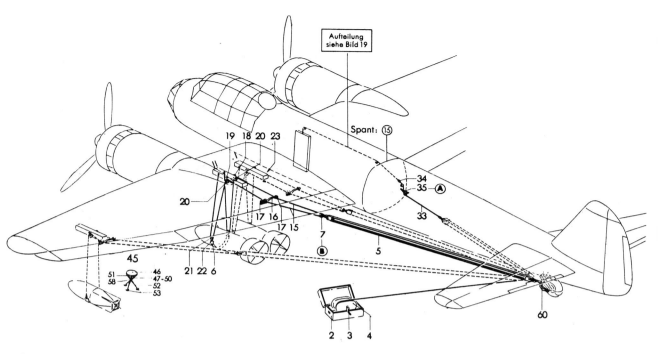

Above: Drawing of bomb loading in the Ju 88 A-5.
Below: Preparing a Ju 88 A-5 for long-distance operations.

Above: A Ju 88 A-5 with an additional FF machine gun and flame extinguishers.

Below: A Ju 88 A-4 with 500-kg bombs and a 600-liter reserve tank.

Above: An operational plane of KG 54 being serviced.

Below: A crash-landed Ju 88 A-5 with shot damage.

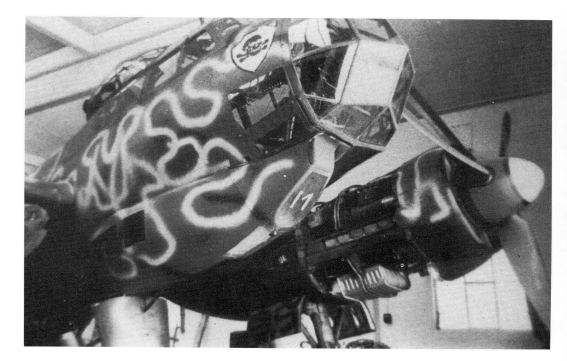

Above: A well-camouflaged Ju 88 A-4 of the 9th/KG 76 during a transfer flight.

Upper right: A Ju 88 A-4 of KG 6 with intense sea camouflage.

Right: A Ju 88 A-4 of KG 54 in 1943.

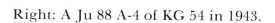

Above: A Ju 88 D-5 reconnaissance plane of the 2nd
(F)/123 in Southern Europe.
Below: A Ju 88 D of the 1st Echelon/ObdL without a belly-pan at Bad
Zwischenahn in 1943.

The Junkers firm produced two test planes, V89 and V90, as forerunners of the Ju 88 H-1. The first bore factory number 430820 and letters RG+RP. In April of 1944 this plane flew with Long-Range Reconnaissance Unit 123 in France. Nine zero-series planes were also delivered to that unit. The H-2 and H-3 series which had also been planned, were canceled early by the RLM.

Test models V23 through V30 were to serve as predecessors of the overworked Ju 88 B-1 to B-3 version, which was readily distinguishable from the Ju 88 A by its aerodynamically redesigned full-visibility cabin. The first of these planes, Ju 88 V23 (D-ARYB), was tested as of June 19, 1940. V24 and V25 served as prototypes for the Ju 88 B-2 and still had Jumo 211 B motors. The Ju 86 V26, the model for the planned Ju 88 B-3 series, had BMW 801 powerplants and was destroyed in May of 1942. Further B-type test models had a modified cabin and redesigned wings. After the cancellation of the B-1 and B-2 production runs, there was a short time when only the Ju 88 B-3 version was planned for production. Junkers intended to arm it with three MG 81 guns.

The Ju 88 V55 and V56 were revised to serve as prototypes for the Ju 88 S-1 series. V55 made its debut on December 28, 1942. The Ju 88 S-1 was a "high-speed bomber" with BMW 801 motors and a maximum bomb load of 900 kilograms. Additional ETC for heavy bomb loads or reserve tanks could be attached under the wings. The S-2 version with its large bomb bay did not go into production. Unlike the S-1, the third S version was equipped with Jumo 213 A powerplants and made to carry a maximum bomb load of 2000 kilograms.

The T-1 and T-3 versions corresponded to S-1 and S-3 respectively except that instead of the bomb-releasing system they now had two serial-photograph cameras built in. The development of the Ju 88 S-4 was halted prematurely; it was to have been an improved S-3 built by Henschel. In March of 1944 Junkers was given a contract to rebuild the Ju 88 S-5 series, but it was soon dropped in favor of night-fighter production. Only one model of the S-5, the Ju 88 V93, was equipped with type TK 1 turbochargers at the end of 1943. The plane was flight-tested at Dessau in mid-March of 1945.

The last successful operations with Ju 88 A-4 and S planes in the West were carried out by the 2nd and 3rd/KG 6, the 1st/KG 66, the 1st and 2nd/KG 54, the 1st/KG 76 and the 1st and 2nd/KG 30.

At the beginning of March 1945 there were only thirty-one Ju 88 S-3 and 138 Ju 88 A-4/14 in action, plus 25 more of the planes in reserve units. There were 51 planes as OKL reserves, while the Luftwaffe had more than 75 Ju 88 A-17 planes. In all, there were scarcely more than 275 of the 13,100 Ju 88 bombers and reconnaissance planes.

Above: The fast low-level attack plane of Captain Lukesch of the 4th/KG 76.

Right: A Junkers Ju 88 S-1 of KG 66 in France.

Upper right and right: Crash-landing of a Ju 88 S-3 of the1st/KG 6, 1944.

Above: A Ju 88 S-1 of KG 66 with black night camouflage on its underside.

JUNKERS JU 188

As the forerunner of the later Ju 188, Junkers presented the Ju 88 E-1 in 1942 in the form of test models Ju 88 V43 and V44, which differed from Ju 88 BV23 through V33 in having larger wing surfaces. A Ju 88 A-4 was rebuilt in 1942 as a prototype for the E-2 version. Its flight testing as the first Ju 88 E-3, with BMW 801 M-2 powerplants, began on April 4, 1942. The next test model, V63, had two Jumo 213 B motors and a rear-mounted HD 151 gun, and flew as of July 1942. After long testing in Rechlin and Tarnewitz, the 63rd test model was in Dessau, well camouflaged, in March of 1945.

The Ju 88 V44 was later designated Ju 188 V1. Testing Command (EK) 188 began to test it and other models in military operations. The zero series was quickly followed by the first series version, called Ju 188 A-2, which was built in early 1944. The A-3 developed from it, was used as a torpedo bomber. The C version was not built because of problems with the remote-control FA 15 rear mantlet. But the Ju 188 D-1 and D-2 did become operational; both were high-speed reconnaissance planes without A-position 151/20 machine guns and a serial photograph system in the tail. Junkers produced the Ju 188 E-1 and E-2 in significant numbers as low-level or torpedo bombers. The latter had no second B-position armament.

Upper right: Mock-up of the Ju 88 B version with three weapon positions.

Right: Ju 88 BV 27 (D-AWLN, factory # 0027) test model at Dessau.

Ju 188 V1 with HL 131Z/1 rear mantlet during testing in Rechlin (September 21-November 23, 1943).

The first Ju 188 with tail guns.

The Ju 188 F-1, likewise powered by two BMW 801 D/G motors, represented the E versions but otherwise corresponded to the Ju 188 D.

Both the Ju 188 G-2 and H-2 were fighters with manned tail guns. Neither the bomber nor the long-range reconnaissance plane went into series production. The fate of the Ju 188 S-1 and T-1 was similar; only a few of the fast S-type reconnaissance planes were built in Leipzig.

It was mainly the Ju 188 A-2, A-3, E-1 and F-1 that were in operations for long periods, particularly with the 1st/KG 6, 1st/KG 66, 1st and 2nd/KG 2, 2nd/KG 26 and Long-Range Reconnaissance Units 120, 122 and 124.

At war's end the Luftwaffe command had only 34 Ju 188 planes in operation, plus six more as OKL reserves. Of them, the Long-Range Reconnaissance Unit (FAGr) 2 had seventeen and FA Gr 3 had fourteen operational planes. On April 26, 1945 only ten Ju 188 remained under Luftwaffe Command 4, with the 3rd (F)/121, plus a few Ju 188 with Air Fleet 6 and in Norway.

Upper right: Repairing a crash-landed Ju 88 B—in Dessau, 1942.

Right: A long-range reconnaissance Ju 188 F-1 of the 4th (F)/14 during compass adjustment.

Above: An operational Ju 188 A-2 plane of the 2nd/KG 6.

Below: A Ju 188 A-2 (U5+PH) bomber of the 1st/KG 2 in France, 1944.

Above: A Ju 188 A-2 of Squadron 6, 1944.

Below: A Ju 188 A-3 LT plane of the 3rd/KG 26 in Norway, 1945.

JUNKERS JU 288

The Ju 288 was supposed to be produced in large series as "Bomber B", a replacement for the now-obsolete Do 217, Ju 88 and He 111. The fact that it was limited to twenty test models and six Ju 288 C-1 planes was attributable, above all, to the lack of high-performance aircraft motors and the general state of the war. Two other planes were presumably scrapped prematurely, while still being built.

The Ju 288 derived from the Junkers EF 73 developmental plane and six very varied project studies with Jumo 222 and 223 motors, a variety of defensive armament and three-seater fuselages.

The first test model (Factory # 0001, D-AACS) made its first flight on November 29, 1940 and was lost in a fire on March 2, 1941. The Ju 288 V2 to V5 were flown a year later. Since the expected Jumo 222 high-performance powerplant was available only in very limited numbers, and very liable to break down as well, both the Ju 288 V1 and V4 were fitted with the weaker BMW 801 motors as an interim solution.

The Ju 288 V5 (BG+GU) was the first prototype fitted with Jumo 222 A/B motors. The subsequent Ju 288 V6 flew as of January 18, 1942 and was finally scrapped by Junkers in October of 1943. The V7 and V8 remained the last test models of the planned A series.

The Ju 288 V9 (VE+QP) represented the first prototype of the Ju 288 B and flew as of April 6, 1942. After a preview in Rechlin on May 11, 1942 came an inclusive test program for the four-seat plane. In March of 1944 the bomber was again available for the Junkers factory to test the Jumo 222 motor. The Ju 288 V10, 11, 13 and 14 test models were assembled, but the V12 was not finished and the V15 and V16 were never completely built.

Above: The second test model of the Ju 288 in Dessau.

Below: Ju 288 V4 (BG+GT, Factory #0004) before its first flight on May 17, 1941.

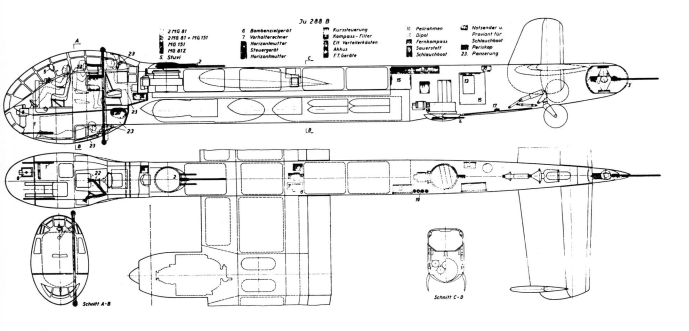

Ju 288 B

1. 2 MG 81
2. 2 MG 81 + MG 151
3. MG 151
4. MG 81Z
5. Stuvi

6. Bombenzielgerät
7. Vorhalterechner
   Horizontmutter
   Steuergerät
   Horizontmutter

8. Kurssteuerung
9. Kompass - Filter
   Elt. Verteilerkästen
   Akkus
   F.T. Geräte

10. Peilrahmen
11. Dipol
12. Fernkompass

    Sauerstoff
    Schlauchboot

    Notsender u.
    Proviant für
    Schlauchboot

22. Periskop
23. Panzerung

Schnitt A-B

Schnitt C-D

Seven test models of the Ju 288 C were built. V101 to V108, of which that with factory number 0105 was not finished. The first model still had DB 606 motors, while from V103 on the heavier DB 610 A/B motors were built in, since the expected Jumo 222 still could not be depended on. The planes with improved powerplants became the forerunners of the few Ju 288 C-1, of which the first was flown in by Holzbauer on December 4, 1943. Until then the instructions of the General Air Ordnance Master and the Marshal of the Reich, stating that the Ju 288 was to go into series production, were still in force. Only after further debacles was the unanimous conclusion drawn early in 1944, that the entire Ju 288 development should be canceled early. After that, Ju 288 V2 to V8, V10, 11, 14, the test models of the Ju 288 C and the first series plane (Factory number 0151) were scrapped. Testing was continued only on Ju 288 V9; the series planes with factory numbers 0153 and 0156 were turned over to the government.

Upper left: Drawing of the Ju 288 B-1 with complete armament.

Left: Ju 288 V11 (Factory #0011, DF+CQ), July 21, 1942.

DEVELOPMENT OF THE 2-ENGINED JU88 DIVE BOMBER

Further development to a high-altitude dive bomber with greatest speed and strongest fighting power.

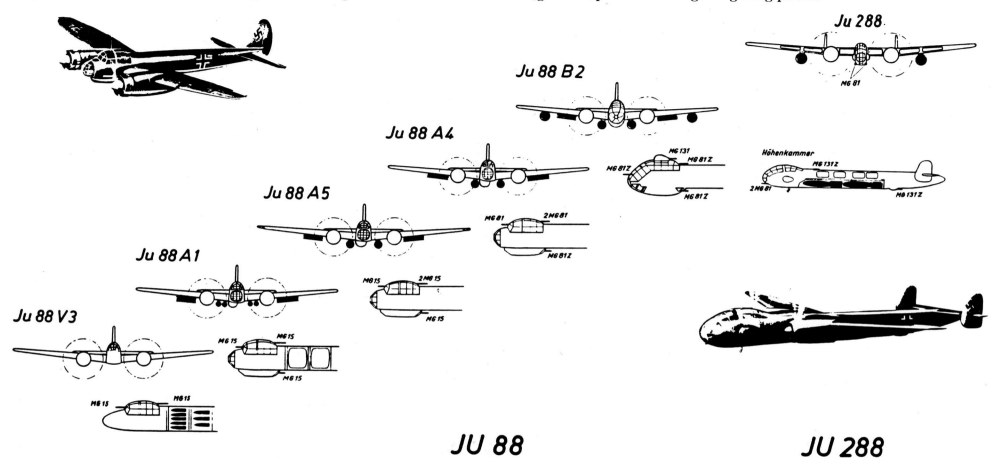

Baumuster		JU 88					JU 288		
		V3	A1	A5	A4	B2		A2	
Motor		Jumo 211A	Jumo 211B	Jumo 211B	Jumo 211J	Jumo 213		Jumo 222	
Bombenlast	kg	16 × 50	1000	1000	1800	2 × 1800	5000	2 × 1800	1800
Flugstrecke	km	1700	2930	4200	3100	2420	2100	3450	4000
Größtgeschwindigkeit	km/h	500	455	465	510	540	640	645	645
Reisegeschwindigkeit	km/h	450	385	400	350	430	575	595	600

37

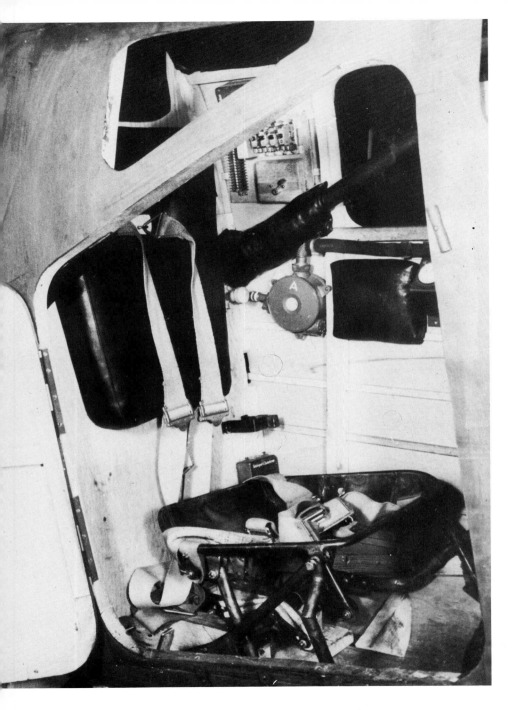

Mock-up of the manned tail-gun position.

The tail-gun position of the later Ju 388 with (here built-out) MG 131 gun.

JUNKERS JU 388

In the search for high-performance high-altitude bombers, the Ju 86 P and R, Do 217 P and Hs 130 A through E had proved to be too slow or too expensive because of their turbochargers. The failure of the Bomber B program also inspired a search for replacement models that could be constructed quickly. In the end a plane based on the production Ju 188 won out. In addition to fifteen test models, some forty finished Ju 388 of the J, K and L versions were built. After the Ju 388 V1 and V2 (PE+IA and PE+IB), both heavy night fighters, there followed several long-range reconnaissance planes and low-level bombers.

The first model of the K-1 production series that was planned later, the Ju 388 V3 (PE+IC), was in Merseburg in April of 1944 and went to Rechlin for testing in January of 1945. The second Ju 388 K-1 was dismantled in Dessau on February 20, 1945 because of a lack of fuel.

The next two prototypes were forerunners of the Ju 368 L-1 construction type, a three-seat high-altitude long-range reconnaissance plane. The factory numbers 500005 and 500006 (PE+IE and PE+IF), the first prototypes, flew at Dessau in the summer of 1944, and some of them were to be seen in Rechlin and Tarnewitz. Fifteen planes were used as zero-series Ju 388 L planes: Ju 388 V7, V8, V10, V12 and V15 plus factory numbers 300291 through 300300 (DW+YY and DW+YZ, DW+ZA through DW+ZH). Late in the summer of 1944 production of the large series of Ju 388 L-1 began in Merseburg, with factory numbers 340081 to 340412. Only some of these planes could be completed, since air raids caused severe damage in central Germany.

Above: Junkers Ju 388 L-1 long-range reconnaissance plane (RT+KD, Factory #340084) during factory testing.

Below: A Ju 388 K-0 model at Magdeburg in 1944.

A few zero-series planes of the bomber version also appeared from July of 1944 on. They were designated KW+TA to BS+TF and bore factory numbers 230151 to 230156.

Some of the test models were made for special uses: Ju 388 V9 (PG+YC), equipped with Jumo 222 motors, or Ju 388 V11, the model of a torpedo bomber. Junkers had Ju 388 V14, 21 and 32 as prototypes with Jumo 213 E motors. To additional Ju 388 L-0 were fitted with DB 603 motors or were tested in practice with K 11 and K 12 automatic pilots. Three Ju 388 long-range reconnaissance planes were also used by the ObdL Test Unit, one each with Jumo 213 E, Jumo 222 and BMW 801 TJ-0 motors. Early in the summer of 1944 it was planned to fly these and some Ju 88 T on reconnaissance in the realm of Attack Leader England as well as in Air Fleets 2 and 3. It is not certain, as has often been asserted, whether Ju 388 L-0 and L-1 were turned over to the ObdL Long-Range Reconnaissance Unit. In any case, one plane of EK 388 was still displayed at Rechlin on November 30, 1944.

The last delivery of Ju 388 planes amounted to two planes in December of 1944. After a few crashes and as a result of enemy action, there were only a few Ju 388 cleared for operations in 1945. For example, test models V4, V7, V9, V14 and V21 were dismantled in Dessau. Only one plane, factory number 340098, was used for oscillation measurement until the war ended.

Upper right: Cockpit of the Ju 388 K-0 before delivery via the Junkers factory in Merseburg.

Right: Ju 388 L-0, factory # 300299, before being rebuilt with DB 603 motors in Munich, 1944.

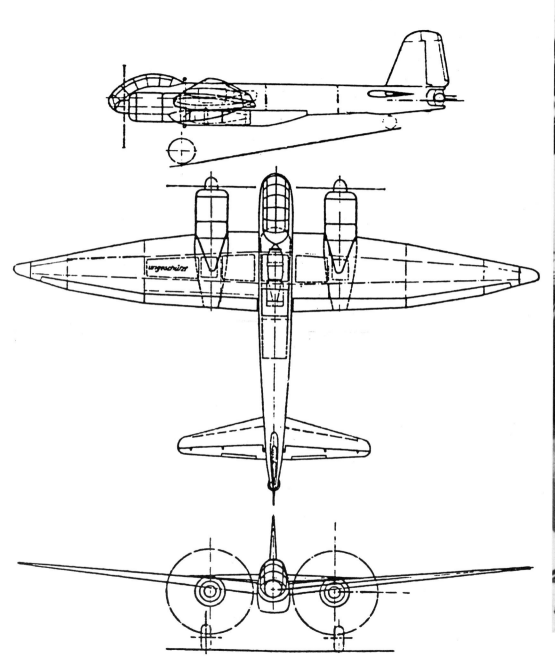

Drawing of the Ju 388 K-0 with large bomb bay.

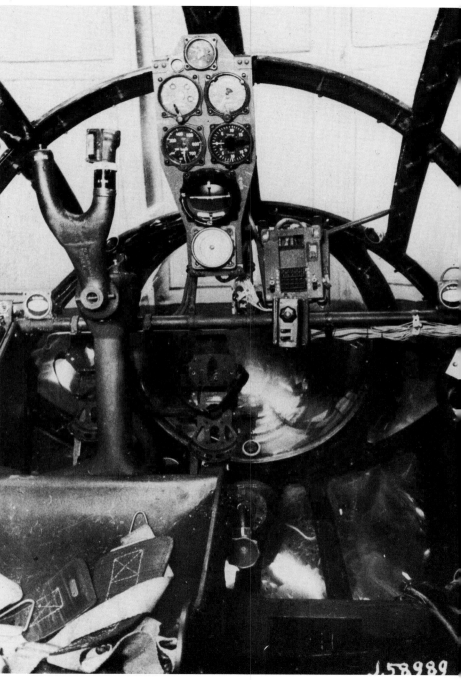

Flight instruments of the Ju 388 L-1.

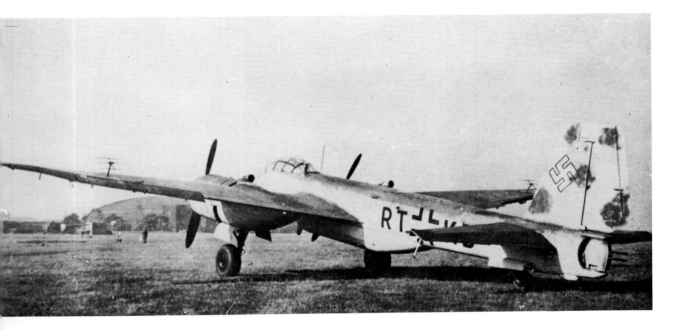

FOCKE-WULF 191

The Fw 191 was one of the participants in the Bomber-B order. As also happened with the competing models, series production at Focke-Wulf failed for lack of sufficiently powerful motors.

At the end of 1940 the final assembly of the first two test models, Fw 191 V1 and V2, took place all the same. In the spring of 1942 Engineer Mehlhorn ran-in both planes. They had been constructed by Engineer Kosel and his colleagues. Instead of two Jumo 222, the planes were powered by only two BMW 801 MA 14-cylinder two-bank radial engines. Since series production remained uncertain, the possibility of equipping the Fw 191, like the Ju 288, with DB 606 or DB 610 motors was considered. The chances of building the Fw 191 B version turned out to be just as slim as those of the Fw 191 C with four individual Jumo 211 F, DB 601 E, DB 605 or DB 628 powerplants.

Only the Fw 191 V6 later received the stronger Jumo 222 A/B motors for testing. Series production of the Fw 191 was canceled because of concurrent work on the Ju 388 K and L.

Upper left: Ju 388 L-1 long-range reconnaissance plane with FL 131 A in tail-gun position.

Lower left: One of the Ju 388 L-1 planes tested at Dessau in 1945.

First test model of the Fw 191 during factory testing
in Hannover-Langenhagen. Servicing and braking of the BMW
801ML powerplants.

MESSERSCHMITT ME 210 AND 410

To replace the Bf 110 fighter-bomber and pursuit bomber, Willy Messerschmitt proposed the Me 210. The planes of production run A-1 were powered by two DB 601 F motors and were 11.2 meters long. According to the factory data presented to the RLM, the plane should be able to carry a maximum bomb load of 2000 kilograms and offer particularly good flying characteristics and performance. The Me 210 A-1 had two MG 17 and two MG 151 as fixed forward armament. The Me 210 B-1 resembled the A-1 only externally, lacking not only the two MG 17 guns but also the bomb-releasing system. Instead there were two serial cameras and flares in the forward bomb bay. A "Destroyer-Stuka", designated Me 210 C-1, was suggested, with DB 605 motors like those of the A-1 and the capability of carrying at most one SC 1800 in its bomb bay. The Me 210 D-1 resembled the C-1 but was set up as a reconnaissance plane. Dr. Wurster made the first flight with the Me 210 V1 on September 5, 1939. The plane was followed by fifteen test models and the A-1 series.

Unfortunately, the hopes for the Me 210 were not fulfilled; the plane was a failure in terms of armament policy.

The Me 410 A-1 was to be an improved Me 210 operating as a "high-speed fighter". The two-seat plane could carry either eight 50-kilogram, two 500-kilogram bombs, or one 1000-kilogram bomb. Two additional ETC could be attached under the wings to hold one SC 50 each. The Me 410 was used in the summer of 1944 as a high-speed fighter and reconnaissance plane by the 1st (F)/23 and 1st (F)/121, 5th/KG 2 and 4th and 5th/KG 51. At the start of 1945 the Me 410 was most often used for scouting by the Long-Range Reconnaissance Units 2 and 3 in the zone of Air Fleet 6 in the East. Most Me 410 planes went first to ZG 26 and were operated almost exclusively as heavy fighters and fighter-bombers in the defense of Germany.

Right: Production of the Me 410 at Dornier-Nord.

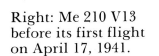

Right: Me 210 V13 before its first flight on April 17, 1941.

Right: Loading an Me 410 with two SC 250 bombs.

Lower right: Me 410 planes decommissioned for scrapping in Southern Germany, 1945.

Below: A crash-landed Me 410 A-1 of the 6th/KG 51 (Factory # 710470).

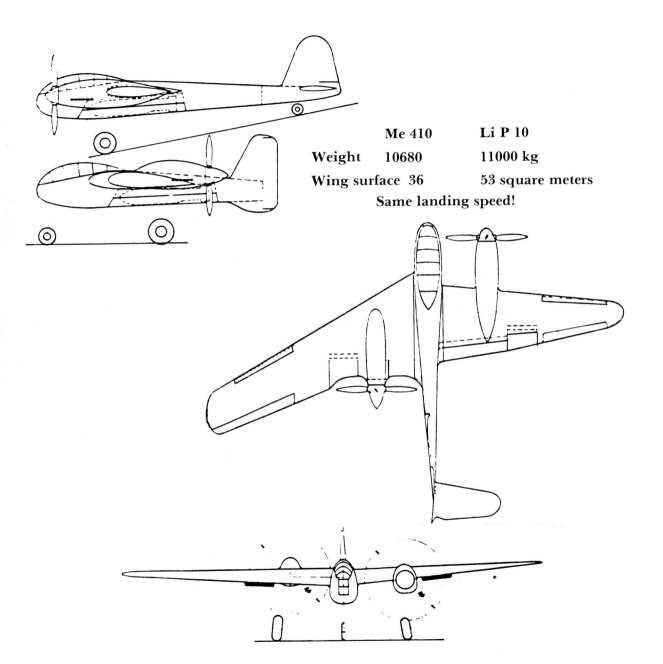

Me 410	Li P 10
Weight 10680	11000 kg
Wing surface 36	53 square meters

Same landing speed!

A comparison drawn by the design department the Messerschmitt firm between the Me 410 and the Li P 10 high-speed fighter plane proposed by Prof. Alexander Lippisch.

DORNIER DO 335

On September 28, 1942 the RLM called for a "highest-speed bomber" and released the necessary specifications. After numerous studies, for example, one involving the Do P 231/1 with DB 605 E motors, the extremely radical design for the Do 335 was created in Friedrichshafen, a high-performance plane with pushing and pulling propellers. As a result of the RLM's lack of a conception, which did not determine whether the Do 335 was needed most as a high-speed bomber, fighter-bomber, night fighter or reconnaissance plane, a great chance was missed. On March 31, 1944 the Ministry postponed the high-speed plane project, only to push it urgently three months later, and then, not long after that, to cancel it in favor of the Dornier night pursuit plane.

As authorized on September 4, 1944 a test command for the Do 335 was set up, chiefly to troop-test the "Mosquito night pursuit plane".

The first Do 335 had long since, as early as October 26, 1943, been run-in by Engineer Dieterle, and 21 further test models were to follow. In the process, the Do 335 V5 (CP+UE) functioned as a weapons-testing plane. In addition a series of ten Do 335 A-0 pursuit bombers (VG+PG to VG+PR, factory numbers 240101 to 240110) was built and used for flight and powerplant testing.

But only very few models of the Do 335 A-1 series version appeared. The same is true of the concurrent training-plane production. On account of the war situation, the Do 435 planned as bombers and long-range reconnaissance planes were never built.

Right: Transporting the Do 335 V1 (CP+UA) to its first flight in Mengen, Württemberg.

Lower right: Loading a Do 335 A-0 at the Dornier factory.

Below: Dornier Do 335 V1 (Factory #230001) during factory testing in Southern Germany.

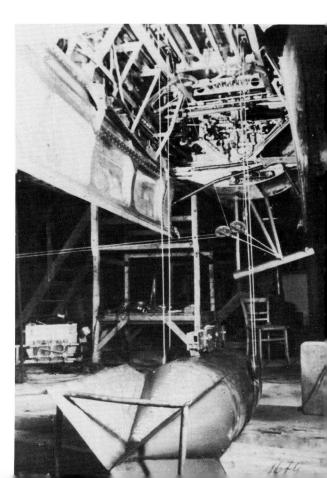

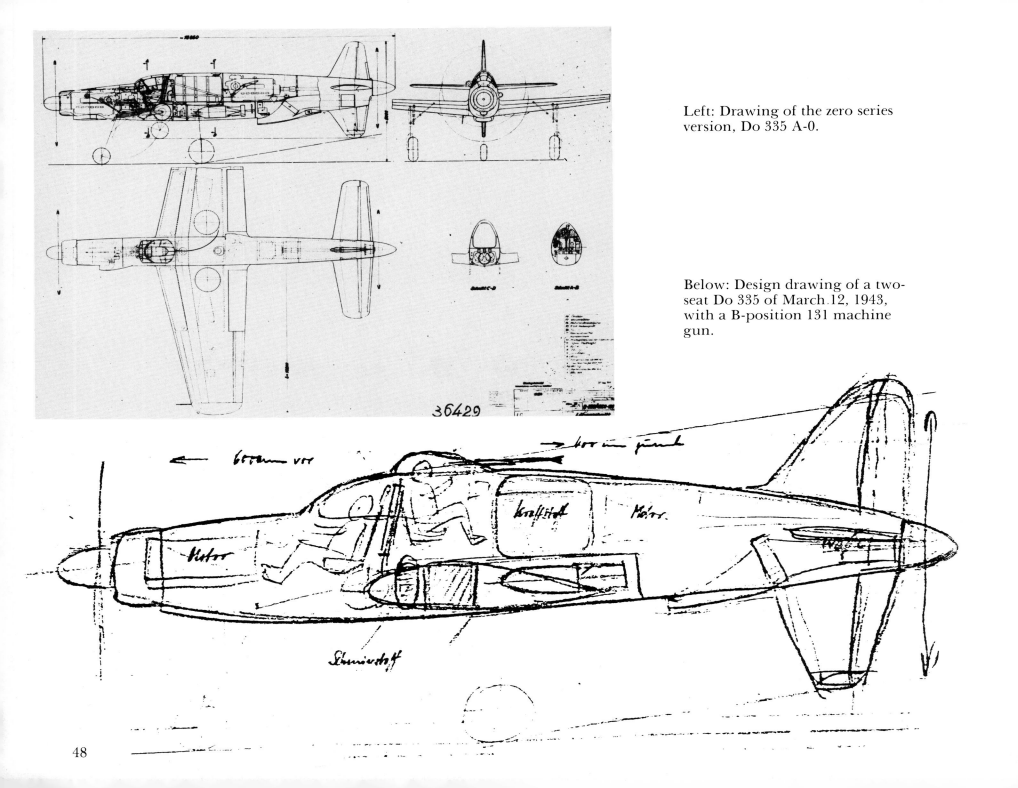

Left: Drawing of the zero series version, Do 335 A-0.

Below: Design drawing of a two-seat Do 335 of March 12, 1943, with a B-position 131 machine gun.

48

MESSERSCHMITT ME 329

In closing, one more Messerschmitt factory project should be examined; it was based on both the Lippisch P 10 and the Me 410, and it resulted in the building of a 1:1 scale wooden mock-up. With the same armament and bomb load (1000 kilograms), the plane, later designated Me 329, was, to be sure, some 360 kilograms heavier than the Me 410, but its speed was calculated to be at most 51 kph faster. In addition, the forward armament was to consist of four 151 machine guns and two MK 103 cannon, with four times 400 or two times 600 rounds of ammunition. The Messerschmitt factory's project description of March 15, 1942 included a copious catalog of the most varied operational uses: heavy pursuit plane, escort fighter, night fighter, armed reconnaissance plane, battle fighter and dive bomber, with up to 2500-kilogram payload. In addition, the inclusion of two 8.8-cm guns for use on the heaviest armored vehicles and shipping targets was considered. For reasons of capacity, the development was filed away as early as the summer of 1942, and preference was given to the Me 410, the conventional construction of which suited the RLM better.

Above and right: Mock-up of the Me 329 in Augsburg. The tail gun built into the empennage is interesting, as is the deployable ladder on the bow.

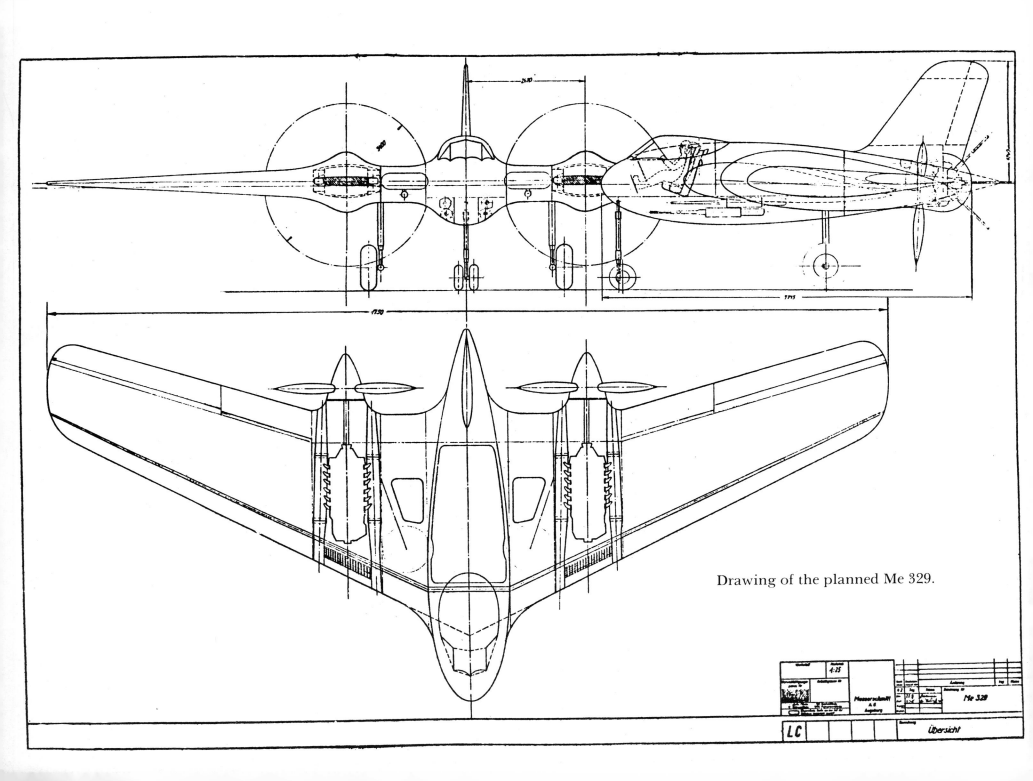

Drawing of the planned Me 329.

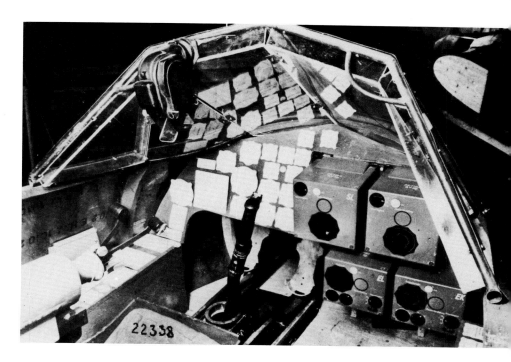

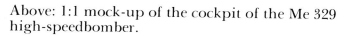

Above: 1:1 mock-up of the cockpit of the Me 329 high-speedbomber.

Above: Interior view of the cabin mock-up.

Below: full-size mock-up of the Me 329 in Augsburg.

Below: Unknown twin-engined high-speed bomber project of 1943.

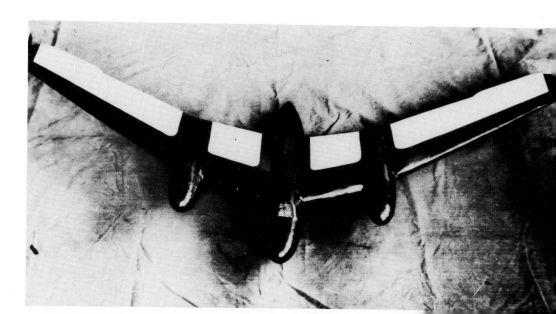

TECHNICAL DATA

Manufacturer	Dornier	Dornier	Heinkel	Junkers	Junkers	Junkers	Junkers	Messer-schmitt	Dornier
Model	Do 17Z	Do 217E	He 111H	Ju 86D	Ju 88A	Ju 188A	Ju 388K	Me 410A	Do 335A
Use	Bomber	Bomber	Bomber	Bomber	Bomber	Bomber	High-level bomber	High-speed fighter	High-speed fighter
Crew	4	4	5	4	4	4	3	2	1
Powerplants	BRAMO 323P	BMW 801ML	Jumo 211F	Jumo 205C	Jumo 211J	Jumo 213A	BMW 801TJ	DB 603A	DB 603D
Wingspan (meters)	18	19	22.5	22.5	20.08	22	22	16.4	13.8
Length (meters)	15.79	18.2	16.2	17.87	14.36	14.95	14.87	12.5	13.85
Height (meters)	4.56	5.03	5.95	5.06	5.07	4.45	4.44	4.3	5
Wing surface (meters)	55	57	87.6	82	54.7	56	56	36.2	38.5
Flying weight (kilograms)	8,890	15,000	14,000	8,060	14,000	14,500	14,300	6,150	7,400
Armament	4-7 MG15	3-5 MG15 1 MG151	1 MGFF 1 MG131 3 MG81Z	3 MG15	5 MG81	2 MG131 2 MG131 1 MG 81Z	HL131	2 MG151 2 MG17	2 MG151 1 MG103
Bomb load (kilograms)	1,000	3,000	3,000	1,000	3,600	3,000	3,000	1,000	1,000
Top speed (kph)	410	420	435	275	440	520	610	620	700
Ceiling (meters)	6,900	7,500	6,700	5,900	8,500	9,500	12,850	9,300	10,500
Range (kilometers)	2,000	2,200	2,900	2,000	2,500	2,400	2,200	1,900	2,150

Left: Ju 88 D-6 with BMW 801+Gml system after its 1000th operational flight with the 1st(F)/120.

Right: He 111 H of the II./KG 54 over the Soviet Union.

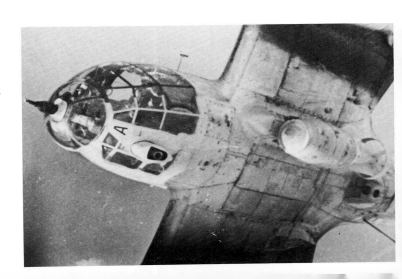